CW01502104

Lock Screen Notification

It took me by surprise
The words.
Your name.
The stereo jingle
Of the reminding
Chiming.

I let it pass by
Like I'd let the day
Pass me by
And I worry that your memory
Might now be
Become
A shadow.

You're not here to remind me
And this reminder needs to not be here.

I remembered.
I always remember.

Birthday.
I'd say happy,
But what's the point
When you're not here
And I'm not happy.

Family

No more lines to draw
For a name borne with pride,
Some of the time.
And lines drawn with pen
Cannot easily be erased.
But the ink all runs dry sometime.

No weight of heritage
For daughters
Sisters
Or wives to bare
Most likely later to forsake this name
And drift as leaves on the wind
Far from this tree.

I am
The last of his name.
I am
My father's son
I am
The apple that fell
Only to drop at the foot
Of a twisted trunk.
I am
Saddened by this falling tree
That in younger days
I would have happily taken
An axe to
Myself.

Everything
Is
Unfinished

SHAUN HARBOUR

ISBN: 9798754528352

Everything is Unfinished (R)

ACKNOWLEDGMENTS

It's been a long, long, weird time of lockdowns, social easing, riding invisible waves and shaking our heads at the denial of science. All the while I've been avoiding writing by pretending that I've been far too busy.

But here is a collection of verse and prose just as weird and liable to leave you shaking your heads.

CONTENTS

Everything is Unfinished (R)

DEDICATION

One day a few years ago the world stood still. Then it changed. Here's to the people and things we managed to hold on to through it all, to those choosing to leave the world changed for the better.

And here's to those who slipped away.

Big Blue Boy Scout

I've drawn you
I've worn you
I tried to be you once upon a time

I watched you
I dreamt you
Beside me as I flew

I read you
I wrote you
I drew your distinct red and blue

I thank Jerry & Joe
(Forever and ever)
I miss Chris & Margot
(Amen)

I lost you
I outgrew you
I know where to find you

When I need you.

The Metaphoric Wreck of Longfellow

Here I stand
The wheelhouse is abandoned
No captain
No navigator
No sextant scanning
Stellar bodies
I'm adrift and afraid of drowning.

Here I lie
No lighthouse
No horizon
Beneath an ash black canvas
Awaiting sparks of ignition
A spark of recognition
Elusive originality
Refusing to answer
To my SOS
No call no text
No SMS
Save
My
Sanity.

Here I end it
No voice
No thought of my own
Face down and empty
Washed onto rocky shores
Tongue tied to a broken mast
A lost son of the Hesperus
Late
Lost and
Longing
For more than just metaphor.
For more than just stolen ideas.

Hurt

Pain
A reminder of life
The remains of lost youth
And the reward for living.
Pain
A collection made over time
A private exhibit
Painted on wounds
Stories of scars inside and out
Only to be shared with those who will recognise such talent.

Pain
Only hurts.

Now memory,

Memory
Opens old wounds
And even time and space
Cannot
Will not
Must not
Stop the pain.

Stop.

Burning the Black Dog

I woke one day feeling blue
And diligently wondered,
"What can I do?"
"What can I do to lift this fog?,
To break this curse?
To chase off this black dog?"

Nothing I could do or say
Could change the way I felt that day
That day, this day the next and more
I felt the dark rise through the floor.
My strength came to a crashing stop
And then, conversely, it did drop
It fell away like a shed snake skin
Revealing the dark and pain within
Except the new skin was just the same
And no one noticed this newborn pain
Such a part of me was it
I wore it well
A perfect fit.

The truth is sometimes you try your best
To whitewash the blue and to divest
Yourself of this weight that drags down hope
To try to feel better to try to cope.

But sometimes the best medicine of all
Is just for a friend to give a call
Just to say "hi" or "ask "how've you been?"
To talk about music, or movies you've seen,
Or anything that isn't the dark
Just to be you again for a moment in time
And for friends to realise you aren't fine
But that's okay
And that's you
Because just to talk about it
And talk through it
To be honest with it
And, to be frank - Fuck it,
Be you
And one day again you'll be back
Because just being you
Is sometimes enough to keep you on track.

Deepest Sympathies

A blank card
A blank slate
I draw a blank

A click of the pen
Pen to paper
A slow march begins to play
With each measured stroke.

I stop
In the middle of my sympathies
And I worry

Selfishly
I wonder
If the words are right
Correct
Soothing

But I know truly
Deep down
That correct and soothing words
Will never fill a hole.
Will never heal a wound
Will never bring them back.

I'm sorry
For your loss

I'm sorry
For your pain

I'm sorry
That you will never feel the same again

I'm sorry
That I can't just
Find the words
To say that.

A Matter Of Faith

No algorithmic calculations
Or stargazing consultations.
No crystal sphere producing visions
Or bag of runes making decisions.
No search with compass, map or sextant
Can hope to find, to any extent
That natural, physical, electric commotion -
That hits every button, of every emotion.

Love comes
When love comes.
It's an answer found in just one sum;
One
Plus one
Equals one.

How Mushroom?

Once
There was a mushroom.
A little happy mushroom
Who happily sat alone,
All day and night.
But the spring brought out the flowers
And within just a few hours
The flowers filled the field
And the colours were a sight.

Now the happy little mushroom
Was lost amongst the flowers
So he filled the noisy hours
With a song.
His song was kind of quiet
And his voice was kind of sweet
But the flowers just swayed and played the whole day long.

His song was sweet.
His song was true.
His song which sang
"I have so mushroom
In my heart for you."

Mushroom stopped his song,
And the days grew rather long,
As the spring turned into summer sunshine cheer.
Then at night the flowers slept
And poor mushroom quietly wept
As he softly sang the song for no one else's ear.

The changing world went on
With no one there to hear his song.
The days slowed down, the summer slowed its pace.
The flowers hung their heads,

As they shivered in their beds.
The cold wind came along and took over the place.

No more song so sweet
No more song so true
No song which sang
"I have so mushroom
In my heart for you."

Along with the winter came the clumping of the cattle
Who stomped and clomped,
While their cow bells rattled,
Til they filled the field with their udders.
The flowers cowered and shook
As the cows took turns to look
And their hungry eyes made little mushroom shudder.

The hungry eyes came with hungry mouths.
The empty bellies came with hungry mouths.
The hungry cows ate and ate all day.
Little mushroom closed his eyes tight.
Little mushroom hoped with all his might
That the chomping sounds would stay far away.

Mushroom thought
his song so sweet
Mushroom imagined
his song so true
Mushroom repeated
and repeated
the song which sang
"I have so mushroom
In my heart for you."

He opened his eyes.

The cows were gone.

He was completely and utterly alone.

All that remained was cow pat after cow pat
And the little lonely mushroom sadly thought that
He would forever be so sad and so alone.
But what was that from the pats he heard?
Not just a sound, not just a word. Not just one voice
But thousands like his very own.

At last he saw with his own tiny, teary eyes
That mushrooms grew, of every size,
Of every shape, and type and kind.
A song rang loud from pat after pat
So the little lonely mushroom sat
With the song rattling round inside his mind.

He knew the tune they sang so true,
That chorus numbering one thousand and two,
He smiled his smile and he sang it too.
"I have so mushroom
In my heart for you."

He smiled because at last he knew he did.

More Or Less

No more, no less
Should you think of me
I now confess
I am enough

I am worth
Your time, respect
No accident of birth
I am love

I don't need
Pity or praise
My epitaph shall read
Simply
"Enough".

Brought To You By the Letter 'F'

I have a favourite word
Four letters
One syllable -
Its guttural
Uttered,
And coarse.
Like a horse hair
Blanket
Enveloping everything
And rubbing everyone
Raw.

Shouted
Sharp.
Screamed
Blue.
Beloved
By me in almost every situation

Subjectively
Adjective
Noun
Verb
A place marking
Punctuation
My favourite word

My favourite
Fucking
Word.

What Happened?

It fell
On the turn of a word
A friendship turned for worse
Their cordiality poured away
In favour of conflict
A chance to inflict
Wounds and nitpick
As any concord
Departed at supersonic speed.
The relationship scuttled
And a heart sunk
The discord palpable
Striking a chord with people
Who can only ask
What.
The.
Fuck.
Happened.
There.

Ablutions

I looked into the misted mirror
And wished I didn't see
The familiar face
Of someone else
Staring back at me

Half shaved I lift the razor
And drew it across my cheek
I watched the clouds
Part ways
I lose
Sight

You're gone
Again.

Buzz

I watched the bee.

The bee watched me
As it buzzed from flower to flower

I think it's worried that I
A giant eye in the sky
Might steal his precious cargo.

Reaper

Inhale
Oxygen travels
Lungs fill as alveoli expand
Deep within
Capillary exchange and
A rush
Of blood refreshed anew
A pulse
Proof of life
Depleted and recycled
The gasp of air
Exhaled
Repeat
Repeat
Repeat
Repeat.
Involuntary.
Instinct.
Life.

The sight of you robs instinct
And takes my breath away
Your touch breaks the cycle
And my heart skips a beat.
So why don't I fear
You,
My beautiful,
Death.

Dementia (demons)

Love.
It hurts.
But for some
Memory fades.
Lost.

Inspiration

Words.
Sometimes
They just don't come.

But sometimes
They roll
And fall
From everywhere

Make and Mend

Nothing broken is unfixable
Except both a heart and a promise

Tenuous Calm

The world was blue and golden bright
As I step out into the light
No footprints mire the path I take
And I pray for all of our sake
That none obstructs this wondrous day
Or my storm may wash them away

The Piskie's Song

When comes the piskies?

When Nature raises a weary hand
To paint the world in shades
Of Autumn

Where come the piskies?

Where the rings of magic
are nearer the world
The piskies dance among
The toadstools

What if I should meet the piskies?

Step carefully
Step quietly
Step quickly
The piskies want to dance.
And they might spirit you away
On a tune
In the wind.

The next poem was an experiment using predictive text and the thinly worn patience of friends. Each person took the time to type the letters of their name into their phones and choose the first word to come up in their predictive text.

Thank you to those friends (listed below) for sharing their unpredictable predictive woes.

I added a few words (in brackets) in order to make some sense of it all.

Thanks to: -

Fraser Cameron

Anne Coldren

Lynne Breckenridge

Susan Turner

Elaine Shaw

Catherine MacFadyen

Fiona Wilson

Mairi MacKintosh

Jan Bell

Laurie Kimborough

Please enjoy...

She/He/They/Gone
(Unpredictable)

[she]
Love and understanding really is everything kind
In my beautiful room.
Oh,
Us getting happy can.
All that he even remembers -
It's now enough

[he]
From right after she even remembers coming (to me),
And my early road,
(To the one I am) on now
For (that) I only needed a wife
I (now) loved someone anew

[they]
Maybe after (all)
It really is just as now

But everything looks like
She used (to)
so am (I) not
Enjoying looking at it now everything

Let you (go)?
No not even.

And no not ever.
[gone]

The Man

The man stood.

He sighed loudly, to no one in particular, took his hands out of his pockets and relaxed. He stared out into the infinite darkness of the void that lay just beyond his reach. His mind wandered as he contemplated the length of eternity and the depth of his emotions. He scuffed his foot in the ether until he felt sand below his shoe. Reaching down he lifted two handfuls of sand and he watched the grains slip through his fingers and blow in small, wisping clouds in the air of his thoughtful sigh. He stared quizzically at the remaining grains that lay in his left hand, and slowly he began to roll them in his hand. He watched intently as the grains rolled and crashed and touched and gathered. All the while he let the sand fall between the motionless outstretched fingers of his right hand. And so time passed. And as time passed he focused on the the rolling crystal grains as they began to cling to each other and dance until eventually he was staring intently at little living marbles of swirling greens and blues and reds and, in the centre, a larger ball made white hot by all the swirling and crashing.
The man held the newly formed sun and moon and universe in the palm of his hand and without a further thought in his head he tossed them all over his shoulder and out into the infinite darkness. Somewhere in the darkness a billion brand new souls drew their first brand new breath. Their joy led to tears, and their tears of joy spun off and filled the infinite darkness with a million billion sparkling lights and the light burned alive for a million years.

The man saw nothing. He sighed loudly, again to no one in particular and continued his empty minded exploration of the infinite void that lay just beyond his reach. He shrugged his shoulders, put his hands in his empty pockets and relaxed.

Hello, my Friend, Hello

A blurry face in the darkness
Framed unnamed
A herald of joy
Loved before
Loved by all
With love for all
From me to you
My friend,
My friends, plus one
Hello.

Remember

They are rebellion
They are honour and pride
They are battle
They are victory
They are loss
They are mourning
They are joy
They are dance
They are memory
They are time and place
They are patriotism

They are remembrance.

Not Like Waves

I burned.
Bright,
Not like a star.
My face was a vision of flame
And smoke -
Human gunfire
An everlasting millisecond
Of carefully judged
Inferno.

No time.
Still,
Not like a moving hand.
Gripped tight to the tiller -
Human nature
Rigidly expounding
Fight or flight.
No time to choose.
No choice.

I fall.
Cushioned,
Not like a pillow.
A parting cloud -
The physical form of air
Here and gone.
Along with the noise
And the terror.

Its over.
Done,
Not like life -
Physics over biology
Science over hope.
The immovable object
Versus
My unstoppable faith that technology
Can beat the odds,
And the stupidity,
Of the other driver.

All safe.
Sound,
Not like a cheer -
A scream, a whisper,
A grateful prayer.
Opportunistically getting word
On high
First come
First served.
First saved.

You're lucky.
Kind of,
Not really -
Broken, but not dead.
Lucky my family is unhurt
Because then I would have done everything
To reverse over
Your luck,
Your outcome,
In less time
Than your last heartbeat.

The crowd returns

I sit in shade.
Hiding from a sun I'm unaccustomed to
A year in hiding.
More.
I watch
People
Real people
No images
No digital mass of pixel
No screen.

Brand new pale white pairs of
Milk bottles topped
With shorts and skirts
Young and old
And all together
A parade of defiance
Defiant but distanced
Militant yet masked

Little old women
With littler, older dogs
Children brimming with enthusiastic innocence
Under baseball cap brims
Pretty pouting pearls
Pouring through doors
In outfits that fit the last time they flit
Around the town.
An unconscious waltz
To the sound of a pounding accordion
changing his tune for change.
Competition ensues
From the previously furloughed tannoys
Of
Every
Open
Shop
Door
The Muzak
Life
Being lived.
Living
Restricted but free.

Play Well in Danish and Collect in Latin

The silent screaming
From the open maw
That empties spewing silence
Into the darkness of
The midnight room.

The searching step
Of a bare sole,
Unshielded and nerves raw
Like a bared soul,
Finds not the safe bed
Of soft woollen pile
Nor the smooth, cool
Underlaid, built for play,
Expanses of vinyl.

Burning through the body,
With a fire that
Fuels
The upward trajectory
Away from the Earth.
Acrylonitrile Butadeine Styrene
Forged in hell.
The sharp unyielding of
A 2x4
A 2x8
And A minifig of Captain America astride a unicorn.

A Park Bench For a Throne, and My Place Upon It

I give my breath to the breeze
And feel the light of the world
As it gently touches my face.

The smells of summer,
The cut grass
And warm tarmac,
The hungover petrichor
From passing gentle showers,
Fill my mind with unseen treasure
And a sense of the world
Turning before me.

The breeze returns my gift of a sigh
And cools my tanning brow.

I close my eyes
Resting and protecting against
The fiery heavens.
To no avail.
And my world is warm and close
And vermilion tinted.

The sounds of life radiate from the parkland
Games and families and
Child's screams of joy
Laughter unabashed and bright as the sun
Is handed to my senses
Like tribute to a golden god.

I am at peace
And I am alive.

This has been

A bit of poetry by

Shaun Harbour

ABOUT THE AUTHOR

Shaun Harbour is a Scottish author and poet who published his first children's book in 2014. Continuing to write he still resides in Perthshire with his wife and daughters.

Printed in Great Britain
by Amazon

42206853R10030